HAL•LEONARD
INSTRUMENTAL
PLAY-ALONG

AUDIO
ACCESS
INCLUDED

PLAYBACK+
Speed • Pitch • Balance • Loop

TROMBONE

Billie Eilish

Audio arrangements by Peter Deneff

To access audio, visit:
www.halleonard.com/mylibrary

"Enter Code"
3554-1886-9973-0051

ISBN 978-1-5400-9213-7

HAL•LEONARD®

Visit Hal Leonard Online at
www.halleonard.com

Contact us:
Hal Leonard
7777 West Bluemound Road
Milwaukee, WI 53213
Email: info@halleonard.com

In Europe, contact:
Hal Leonard Europe Limited
42 Wigmore Street
Marylebone, London, W1U 2RN
Email: info@halleonardeurope.com

In Australia, contact:
Hal Leonard Australia Pty. Ltd.
4 Lentara Court
Cheltenham, Victoria, 3192 Australia
Email: info@halleonard.com.au

CONTENTS

BAD GUY

TROMBONE

Words and Music by BILLIE EILISH O'CONNELL
and FINNEAS O'CONNELL

I LOVE YOU

TROMBONE

Words and Music by BILLIE EILISH O'CONNELL
and FINNEAS O'CONNELL

EVERYTHING I WANTED

TROMBONE

Words and Music by BILLIE EILISH O'CONNELL
and FINNEAS O'CONNELL

Idontwannabeyouanymore

TROMBONE

Words and Music by BILLIE EILISH O'CONNELL
and FINNEAS O'CONNELL

LOVELY

TROMBONE

Words and Music by BILLIE EILISH O'CONNELL,
FINNEAS O'CONNELL and KHALID ROBINSON

NO TIME TO DIE

TROMBONE

Words and Music by BILLIE EILISH O'CONNELL
and FINNEAS O'CONNELL

Slowly, mysteriously

OCEAN EYES

TROBMONE

Words and Music by
FINNEAS O'CONNELL

YOU SHOULD SEE ME IN A CROWN

TROMBONE

Words and Music by BILLIE EILISH O'CONNELL
and FINNEAS O'CONNELL

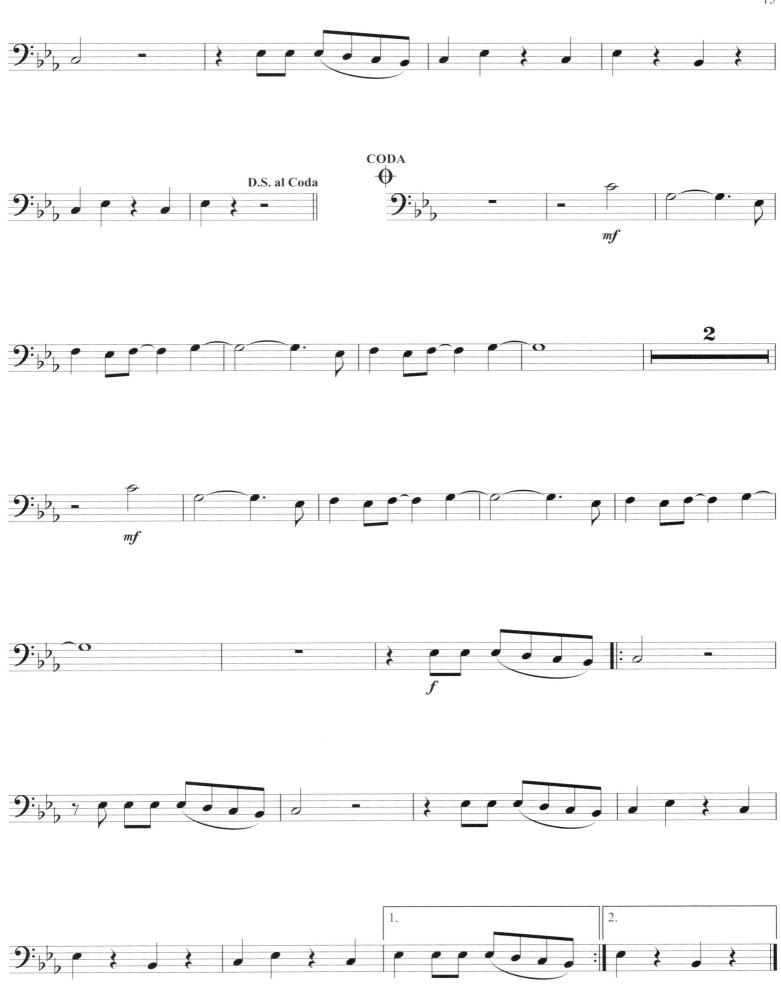

WHEN THE PARTY'S OVER

TROMBONE

Words and Music by
FINNEAS O'CONNELL